enjoy your meal

What Happens To Your Food When You Eat?

Emily McGregor

Rourke

Publishing LLC

Vero Beach, Florida 32964

www.rourkepublishing.com

PHOTO CREDITS: p. 9: Diego Alvarez de Toledo/istockphoto.com; p. 17: Daniel
Brunner/istockphoto.com; p. 28: BSIP Estiot/Science Photo Library; pp. 5, 14: Ronnie
Comeau/istockphoto.com; pp. 6, 23, 33, 35: Discovery Picture Library; p. 29: Edwin
Ellis/Agnieszka Steinhagen/istockphoto.com; p. 40: Chris Fairclough/CFWImages.com;
title page, pp. 10, 12, 36, 39: Chris Fairclough/Discovery Picture Library; p. 16: Liv Friis-
Larsen/istockphoto.com; p. 43: John Giustina/Getty Images; p. 22: Andy Green/
istockphoto.com; pp. 4, 13, 21: istockphoto.com; p. 25: Zak Kendal/Getty Images;
p. 38: Stephen Morrison/Corbis; p. 19: Thomas Polen/istockphoto.com; p. 41: Andy
Sacks/Getty Images; p. 34: Chris Schmidt/istockphoto.com; p. 42 (both): Suzannah
Skelton/istockphoto.com; pp. 20, 24: Agnieszka Steinhagen/istockphoto.com;
p. 31: James A. Sugar/Getty Images.

Cover shows a selection of healthy vegetables [Andy Green/istockphoto.com].

Produced for Rourke Publishing by Discovery Books
Editors: Geoff Barker, Amy Bauman, Rebecca Hunter
Designer: Ian Winton
Cover designer: Keith Williams
Illustrator: Stefan Chabluk
Photo researcher: Rachel Tisdale

Library of Congress Cataloging-in-Publication Data

McGregor, Emily..
  Enjoy your meal : what happens when you eat? / Emily McGregor.
    p. cm. -- (Let's explore science)
  Includes index.
  ISBN 978-1-60044-603-0
  1. Digestion--Juvenile literature.
  QP145 .M23 2008
  612.3 22
                              2007020105

Printed in the USA

CONTENTS

CHAPTER ONE
GETTING STARTED

Your **stomach** is rumbling. You know you need to eat. But what happens to the food once you have eaten it? In this book, we will look at the journey your food takes through your body.

Food gives you energy. Without food you would not be able to run and play.

You put food in your mouth and chew it. This starts the food on its journey through your body.

Into Your Body

Everyone needs food. Food contains **nutrients** that keep you alive and healthy. Nutrients are important chemicals in food. When you eat food, your body works hard to **absorb**, or soak up, the nutrients. Most food is absorbed in your **small intestine**. The small intestine is a very long tube.

What Is Digestion?

Digestion is the process of breaking down large pieces of food into smaller pieces and absorbing them. The smaller the pieces of food, the more easily your body can absorb them. Most digestion happens in your small intestine. But it also takes place in your mouth and in your stomach.

Bread is an everyday food in many countries. Bread contains starch. Enzymes in your mouth break down starch.

How Is Food Broken Down?

In your mouth, you chew food into smaller pieces. When it enters the stomach, the stomach churns it around. This breaks it into smaller pieces, too. Chemicals in your body also help break down food.

Your body contains many chemicals. Each has its own job. In digestion, the chemicals that break down food are called **enzymes**. Different enzymes break down different types of food. For example, one enzyme called amylase breaks down starch. Starch is a nutrient found in bread. Another enzyme breaks down protein. Protein is a nutrient found in meat.

How Do Enzymes Work?

Enzymes speed up chemical reactions. Starch is a nutrient and a big chemical. An enzyme amylase helps break starch down. The enzyme speeds up the reaction that chops the starch into smaller pieces.

How Do We Use Broken Down Food?

Once the food is broken down, the body absorbs the smaller nutrients. The nutrients help us grow. They keep our bodies healthy and functioning normally.

Chopping Food Into Smaller Pieces

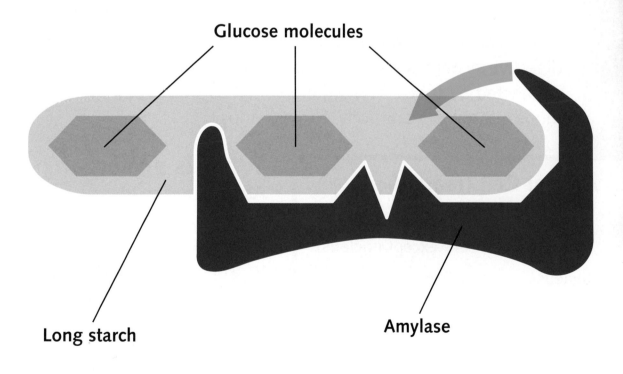

Glucose molecules

Long starch

Amylase

Enzymes are able to speed things up in the body. A special enzyme in the mouth, amylase, helps break down starch into smaller pieces (glucose molecules).

CHAPTER TWO

WHERE DOES FOOD GO WHEN YOU EAT?

When you eat, food enters your **digestive system**. Your digestive system is a series of hollow **organs**. They are connected by tubes. This system stretches from your mouth, through your body, to your anus.

Animal Cell (magnified)

Cytoplasm (contents of cell, except nucleus)

Nucleus (central part)

Cell membrane (layer)

An animal cell.

What Is an Organ?

Animals are made of millions of tiny **cells**. The cells group together to form body **tissues**. Tissues are collections of cells that carry out similar roles. They group together to form organs. Your skin is an organ. It is made of groups of tissues. The tissues are made of cells.

CELLS ARE THE BUILDING BLOCKS

- Scientists estimate that the human body has up to 100 **trillion** cells.
- Your skin is your largest organ. Imagine that the skin of an adult person could be stretched out flat. It would cover two square yards (1.7 square meters). That much skin would weigh about nine pounds (4 kilograms).

Your largest organ—skin—can be damaged by sunlight. Remember to use sunscreen to keep yourself safe.

Which Organs Form My Digestive System?

The following organs are part of your digestive system:

1. mouth
2. **esophagus**
3. stomach
4. small intestine
5. **large intestine**

Each organ is connected to the next by tubes.

The Long Journey

When you eat, the food first enters your mouth. You chew and swallow the food. It moves down your esophagus. Next, it enters your stomach. From your stomach, it moves down into your small intestine. Then, it passes into your large intestine. Later, it moves into the **rectum**. It passes out of the body through the anus.

How Long Does the Journey Take?

Your food spends time in each part of your digestive system. At each step, food is digested. Any undigested food passes right through the digestive system and out of the anus.

- Mouth: Food stays in your mouth for about ten seconds.
- Esophagus: Food takes five to six seconds to move down your esophagus.
- Stomach: How long food stays in your stomach depends on the food. Most food stays in the stomach between two and four hours.
- Small intestine: The food takes from five to six hours to pass through the small intestine.
- Large intestine: The food takes from twelve to twenty-four hours to pass through the large intestine.

In total, food takes from twenty to thirty hours to pass through your body.

Food stays in your mouth for a very short length of time. But chewing food is an important part of digestion.

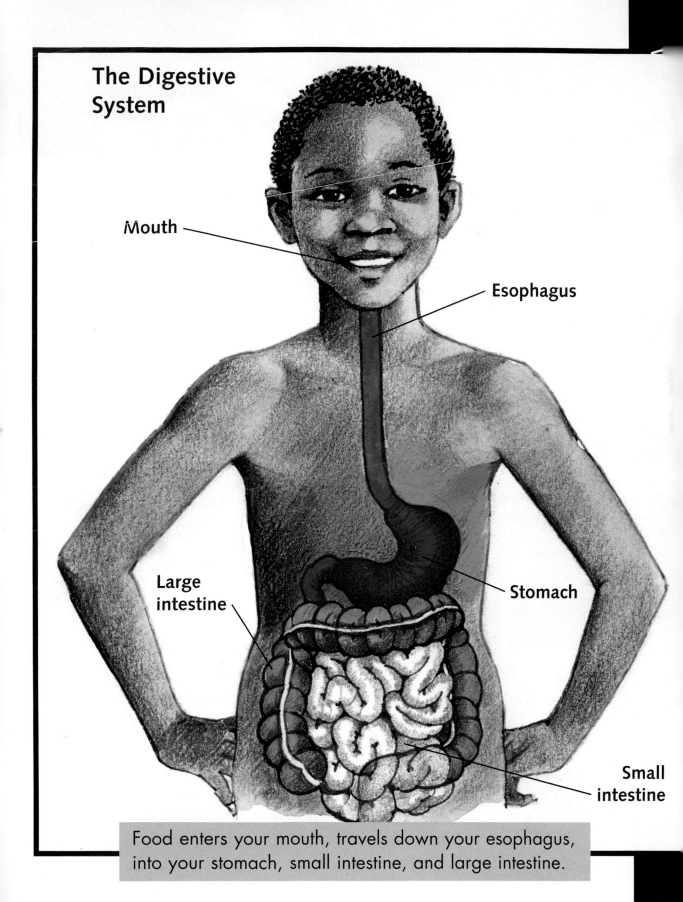

The Digestive System

Mouth

Esophagus

Stomach

Large intestine

Small intestine

Food enters your mouth, travels down your esophagus, into your stomach, small intestine, and large intestine.

CHAPTER THREE

WHAT HAPPENS IN MY MOUTH?

Your mouth is your first digestive organ. You eat because you are hungry and because you enjoy the taste of food. Most people are attracted to certain foods by the smell. Everyone enjoys some foods. Everyone also has foods they do not like.

Why Is My Tongue Important?

Your tongue detects the taste of food. Your tongue's main job is to protect you from poisonous or rotten food. You would spit out a food if it tasted really bad!

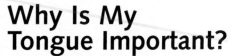

Your tongue tastes sweet ice cream. It can also tell you that the ice cream is cold.

Taste buds cover your tongue. Taste buds detect tastes. There are four main tastes:

- bitter
- sweet
- salty
- sour

A TONGUE FULL OF TASTE BUDS

Your tongue has many taste buds on it. There may be as many as 10,000! Each taste bud has up to 100 cells that detect taste.

If you licked a lemon, it would taste very sour.

What Does Smell Have To Do With It?

Most foods don't have just four tastes. To taste a full range of flavors, you need a sense of smell. So your nose and mouth are connected. Without your sense of smell, you would not be able to taste your food very well. You can try this for yourself. Hold your nose the next time you eat some food. Can you still taste it?

Why Do I Have to Chew Food?

Food must be broken down. Chewing food with your teeth breaks the food down. Large pieces of food break down into smaller pieces of food. Your tongue plays an important part in chewing. You move food with your tongue. Then you bite down on the food with your teeth.

Teeth

Babies have twenty teeth. Adults have thirty-two teeth. Your front teeth are called your incisors. The next teeth are called the canines. You use these two types of teeth to bite and tear food. The teeth at the back and sides of your mouth are called premolars and molars. Most chewing is done on these large teeth.

Baby teeth fall out to make way for adult teeth.
Can you remember when your baby teeth fell out?

First Teeth

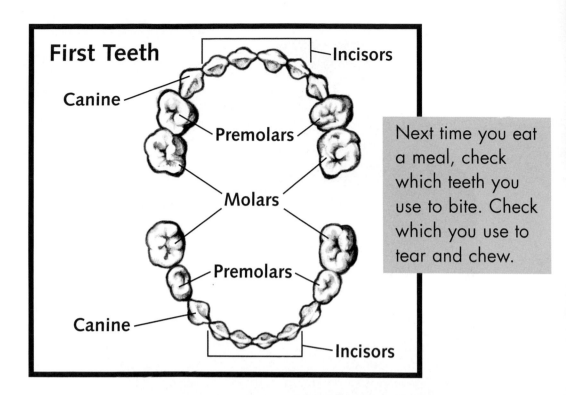

- Incisors
- Canine
- Premolars
- Molars
- Premolars
- Canine
- Incisors

Next time you eat a meal, check which teeth you use to bite. Check which you use to tear and chew.

Tooth Decay

If you do not regularly brush your teeth, food collects on them. **Bacteria** feed on the food. They make acids. The acids eat away at your teeth. This can cause teeth to **decay**. You can prevent tooth decay by brushing your teeth regularly.

Teeth are covered with a hard substance called enamel.

Cutaway of a Tooth

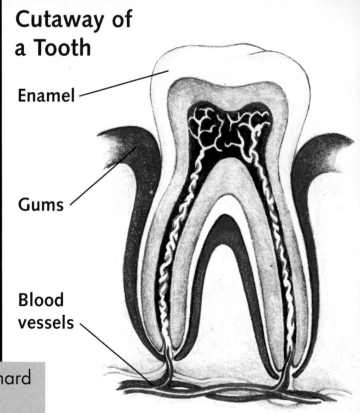

- Enamel
- Gums
- Blood vessels

Does this photograph make your mouth water? Saliva forms in your mouth when you are ready to eat.

Why Does My Mouth Water?

Think about your favorite food. Does it make your mouth water? When your mouth waters, you are making **saliva**. Saliva is a watery liquid. You make it in your mouth all day long. You need saliva for three main reasons:

1. To make food wet. It is hard to swallow food dry. Imagine eating a cracker or a sandwich without saliva to make it moist. It would be very hard to do. Also, your tongue can not taste food when it is dry. Saliva helps you taste.

2. To help keep your mouth clean. Saliva rinses the inside of your mouth. It contains chemicals that help prevent infection.

3. To begin the process of digestion. Saliva contains enzymes. An enzyme in saliva digests starch. Starch is found in food like bread and pasta.

ALL DAY, EVERY DAY

Your mouth makes saliva twenty-four hours a day. You make about two pints (one liter) of it every day!

What Is Saliva?

Saliva is 98 percent water. It also contains mucus, enzymes, and other chemicals. Saliva is made by **glands**. The glands are found in the bottom and sides of the mouth.

It would be hard to swallow food without saliva. Babies produce plenty of saliva too!

How Do I Swallow?

You chew your food. As you do, you mix it with saliva. Your tongue pushes the wet ball of food to the back of your mouth. It enters the esophagus. The esophagus is a hollow tube of muscle. It squeezes the ball of food. This pushes the food downward.

Imagine you squeeze a tube of toothpaste. You squeeze at the end and push toward the opening. The toothpaste comes out the other end. The esophagus works in a similar way. In the esophagus, rings of muscle squeeze the food. They push it toward the stomach.

Moving Food Toward the Stomach

Esophagus

Area of squeezing

Ball of food

Muscles in the esophagus squeeze food downward.

You can swallow even if you are upside down. That's because the esophagus is strong. It can push food toward the stomach no matter which end is up. The food slides down easily because it is wet. If the food is dry, it does not move down as easily.

A LONG WAY DOWN

A human esophagus is about 10 inches (25 centimeters) long. A giraffe's is much longer. It runs up the giraffe's 6-foot (1.8-m) neck. With it, the giraffe can regurgitate food. This means it brings food back into its mouth. The food moves from the bottom of the esophagus to the top. Then the giraffe chews the food again. This helps with its digestion.

CHAPTER FOUR

WHY DO I HAVE A STOMACH?

Your stomach is at the end of your esophagus. Food comes into the stomach from the esophagus. The stomach is a bag made of muscle. It breaks down large food chemicals into smaller food chemicals.

Your stomach is part of your digestive system. It is at the end of your esophagus.

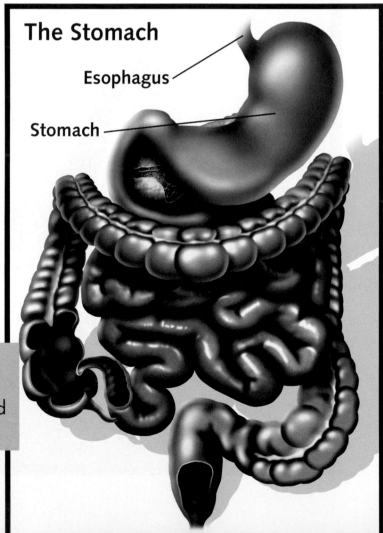

The Stomach

Esophagus

Stomach

BUSY STOMACH

Cows have four stomachs! They need extra stomachs because they eat only grass. Grass is difficult to digest. Digesting it takes a long time.

How Big Is My Stomach?

The size of your stomach changes when you eat. After a meal, it holds about 2 pints (1 liter) of food. It can hold more than 8 pints (4 liters) of food! But that would be very uncomfortable.

What Does the Stomach Do?

The stomach has three jobs:
1. It stores food.
2. It breaks down food into a liquid mixture. The liquid mixture is like a thick cream. To break the food down into a liquid, the stomach squeezes and squashes the food inside it.
3. It slowly moves food into the small intestine.

Are There Enzymes in the Stomach?

The stomach has enzymes. The enzymes help break down protein. Protein is found in some foods such as meat. Enzymes are not the only chemicals in the stomach. The stomach makes other juices, too. These include acid and other chemicals that help with digestion. The stomach mixes the food with the juices. The juices also help kill any harmful bacteria in the food. This keeps us from getting sick.

Enzymes in the stomach help break down protein. Protein is found in bacon, sausages, and beans.

Why Doesn't the Stomach Digest Itself?

Stomach juices are very acidic. You might think that these juices could harm the stomach. But they do not. The stomach is protected by a thick lining.

INDIGESTION

Have you ever had pain in your stomach after eating? This could be **indigestion**. Eating a big or rich meal can cause it. Then, acid from the stomach splashes up the esophagus. It gives you a burning feeling.

This is sometimes called **heartburn**. But it has nothing to do with the heart. For help, you take a thick and creamy medicine. The medicine sits on top of the stomach acid. This stops it from splashing up the esophagus.

Why Does My Stomach Rumble?

Your stomach rumbles when you are hungry. Your stomach is always moving and squeezing its contents. There is a ring of muscle at the top of the stomach. There is another ring at the bottom. Air can enter the stomach when the top ring of muscle opens. Sometimes the stomach squeezes air instead of food. Then, it starts to make noises. This is your stomach rumbling. It's time to eat!

How Does Food Leave the Stomach?

Food stays in your stomach when the small intestine is full. But soon there will be space in the small intestine again. Then, the bottom ring of muscle opens. It lets out small amounts of the runny liquid food.

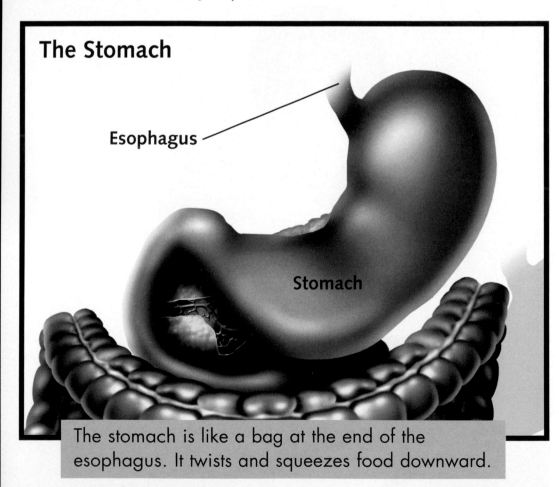

The Stomach

Esophagus

Stomach

The stomach is like a bag at the end of the esophagus. It twists and squeezes food downward.

WATER

Food is not all we need to survive. Water is very important, too. Our bodies are two-thirds water. We can not live longer than three or four days without water. We get about 20 percent of the water we take in every day from our food.

CHAPTER FIVE

WHAT IS GOING ON IN MY INTESTINES?

Humans have two types of intestines. One is the small intestine, and one is the large intestine. Each has a different job. But both are important. They make up the final steps of digestion.

The Small Intestine

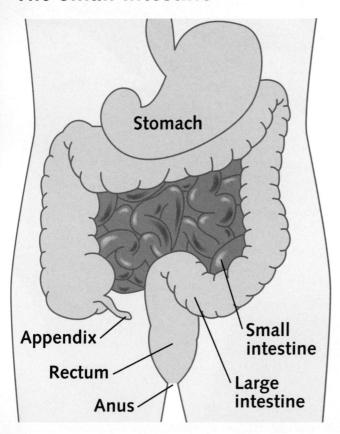

Stomach

Appendix

Rectum

Anus

Small intestine

Large intestine

The small intestine lies beneath the stomach. Food from the stomach comes here.

A Closer Look at the Small Intestine

After food is broken up in the stomach, it moves into the small intestine. By this time, it has been broken down into small chemicals. The small intestine can handle small chemicals more easily than large chemicals.

The small intestine is a long, narrow tube. It is about 2 inches (5 cm) wide. It is curled around and around beneath your stomach. If you stretched out an adult's small intestine, it would be about 23 feet (6.7 m) long.

How Long?

23 feet (6.7 m)

The small intestine is about 23 feet (6.7 m) long. That's about the height of four men standing on top of each other.

What Is the Small Intestine's Main Job?

The small intestine breaks down food even more. By the end of the small intestine, the food is broken into tiny chemicals. These can be absorbed (soaked up) into the blood.

AIDING DIGESTION

The liver, gall bladder, and pancreas are three vital organs. They aid digestion in the small intestine. The liver has many important functions (see also page 31). One of the important things it does is to make a liquid called bile.

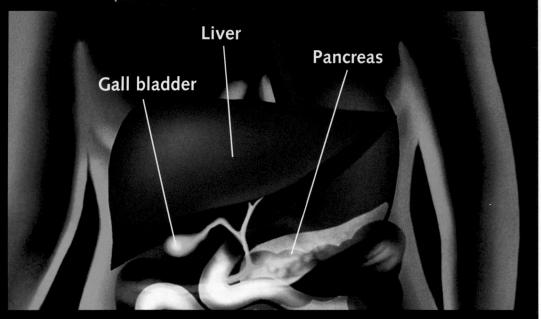

Liver

Pancreas

Gall bladder

More Juices!

For the small intestine to work well, it needs more juices. Three organs produce juices that help digestion. They send the juices into the small intestine. These organs are:
- The liver
- The gall bladder
- The pancreas

What do they do?
- The liver makes a liquid called **bile**.
- The gall bladder stores bile until it is needed. Bile helps your body absorb fat into the bloodstream.
- The pancreas makes juices that help the body digest fats and protein.

The Problem with Fat

Fat is hard for your body to break down. Have you ever tried cleaning a greasy pan? If you have, you know it is hard to get the fat off. When you add detergent, the fat breaks into smaller pieces. Then it is easier to wash away. Bile works in a similar way. It is held in the gall bladder until you eat a fatty meal. Then it is released into the small intestine. It breaks down fat.

Fats such as butter and animal fats need breaking down. This happens in the small intestine.

How Are Nutrients Absorbed?

Soon your food reaches the end of the small intestine. Then, it is ready to be absorbed. The inside of the small intestine is covered with millions of tiny "fingers." These fingers are called **villi**. The villi make the surface area of the small intestine a lot bigger. If the small intestine had smooth walls, it could not absorb as many nutrients. A big surface area means more food can be absorbed. Food crosses the villi. It enters the bloodstream.

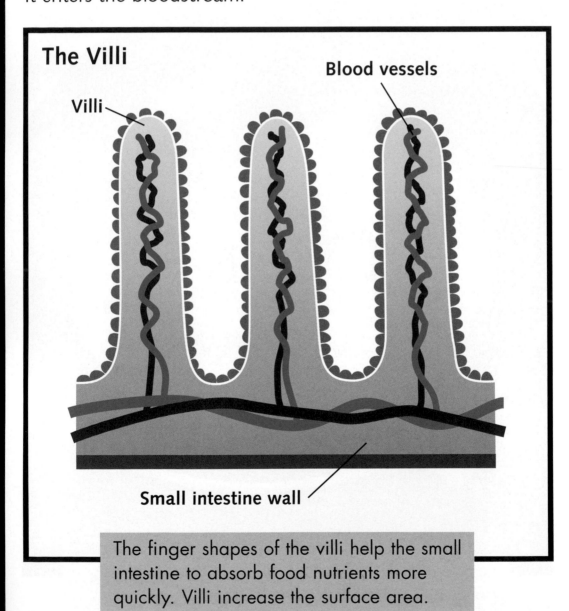

The Villi

Villi

Blood vessels

Small intestine wall

The finger shapes of the villi help the small intestine to absorb food nutrients more quickly. Villi increase the surface area.

AMAZING INSIDES
Imagine the villi could be laid out flat. They would cover an area of 240 square yards (200 sq m). That's about the size of a tennis court!

Where Does the Food Go Next?
The blood is rich in nutrients from food. It goes straight to the liver. The liver takes harmful matters out of the blood. For example, if someone has drunk alcohol, the liver removes the alcohol.

The liver stores some nutrients. It will release these later when they are needed. It sends other nutrients to different parts of the body.

A Closer Look at the Large Intestine

The large intestine gets rid of waste food. Not all of your food is absorbed. The body does not need some of it. This is the waste. It leaves the small intestine and moves into the large intestine. The large intestine is wider than the small intestine. It is 3–4 inches (7–10 cm) wide and 5 feet (1.5 m) long.

The Large Intestine

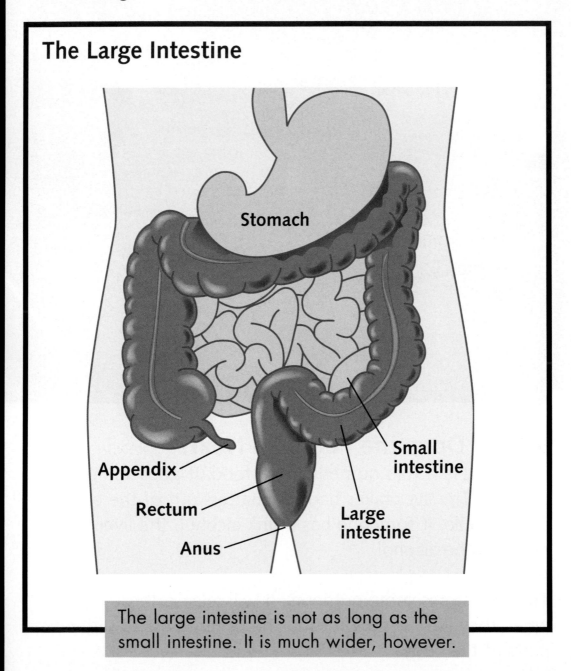

The large intestine is not as long as the small intestine. It is much wider, however.

TIME TO GO

It is important to eat a diet rich in fiber. Fiber is found in plants. It adds bulk to your feces, or waste matter. Eating fiber helps you get rid of waste regularly. By eating fiber, you keep your large intestine healthy.

What Happens in the Large Intestine?

At the start of the large intestine, the food is runny. Water is absorbed back into the body as it moves along. This happens in a part of the large intestine called the colon. The food waste, or feces, becomes harder. They become solid as they move through the large intestine.

Eventually, they reach a storage area. This is the rectum. From there, the feces leave the body through the anus.

CHAPTER SIX

WHY DO I NEED FOOD?

All animals need food to survive. Food gives us energy to carry out the four main life processes. These are:

- Movement: Animals usually move their whole bodies.
- Growth: All animals grow from a baby to an adult.
- Reproduction: Animals can give birth to young.
- Nutrition: Animals take in food. This provides energy for all four processes.

Animals get their energy from food. The young can then grow to become adults.

Today's food will become tomorrow's cells in your body. It is important to eat a balanced, healthy diet.

How Much Food Do I Need?

At different times of life, humans need different amounts of food. The more energy you use, the more food you need to eat. For example, athletes use lots of energy. So they need a lot of food. Older people do not use as much energy. So, they need less food. But whatever your age, you need a balanced diet.

What Is a Balanced Diet?

A balanced diet is one that contains the six main food types. These are carbohydrates, proteins, fat, vitamins, minerals, and fiber. And, of course, everyone needs water. The foods must be eaten in the correct amounts. You would not be healthy if you ate a diet full of fat!

Why Do I Need All Six Food Groups?

The table below shows the kinds of food in each food group. It also shows you why you need each food group.

Food Type	How Do I Get It?	Why Do I Need It?
Carbohydrates (starch)	Bread, pasta, rice, cereals	For energy
Carbohydrates (sugar)	Cakes, cookies, candies	For energy
Protein	Meat, fish, eggs	For cell growth and repair
Fat	Butter, oil, cheese, milk, meat	For energy
Vitamins and minerals	Vegetables, fruit, dairy products	For cells
Fiber	Cereals, fruit, vegetables	For a healthy digestive system

KEEPING FIT

It is important to eat a balanced diet. To keep healthy, it is also very important to exercise. Walk the dog, play soccer with your friends, or join a sports club. There are hundreds of ways to stay fit!

How To Eat a Balanced Diet

The food pyramid shows you how much of each food group to eat. If you follow this pyramid, you will be doing your best to keep healthy.

The Food Pyramid

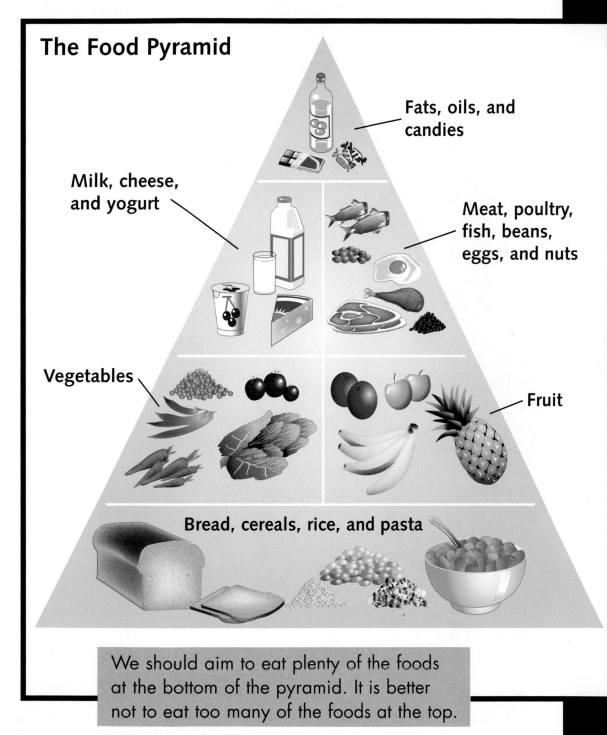

Fats, oils, and candies

Milk, cheese, and yogurt

Meat, poultry, fish, beans, eggs, and nuts

Vegetables

Fruit

Bread, cereals, rice, and pasta

We should aim to eat plenty of the foods at the bottom of the pyramid. It is better not to eat too many of the foods at the top.

And If I Don't Eat a Balanced Diet?

Without a balanced diet, you may get sick. Some diseases are caused when a person does not eat from all of the food groups. These diseases are rare in developed countries like the United States.

Scurvy

People get scurvy when they do not get any vitamin C. Vitamin C is found in fruits and vegetables. Oranges, lemons, and limes are the best source of vitamin C. People with scurvy have bleeding gums, painful joints, and bad skin. These can be cured by eating vitamin C.

Many people do not get a balanced diet. Some may even die of starvation.

Keep an eye on what you eat. Eat plenty of fruit and vegetables to keep healthy.

Rickets

People who do not get any vitamin D can get rickets. Vitamin D is found in some fish, eggs, and dairy products. When children have rickets, their bones do not grow properly. Rickets is treated by giving the patient vitamin D and calcium. Calcium is found in milk.

Feeling Healthy

These diseases are rare. But it is important to eat a balanced diet to feel healthy. If your diet lacks a food group, you may feel tired. You may have less energy. You may not be able to think clearly. By eating all of the food groups, you make sure you have all the nutrients that you need.

What you eat is important. But how much you eat is also important.

What Happens If I Eat More Than I Need?

Your body uses the energy in food. Some people eat more food than they need. The body stores the extra food as fat. The fat is found under the skin. If someone has too much body fat, they are said to be **obese**. Being obese can cause problems. Obese people are more likely to have heart problems. They are also more at risk of other diseases, such as cancer and diabetes.

It is harder to carry around a lot of extra weight. It can also cause plenty of health problems.

What Happens If I Eat Less Than I Need?

If you do not eat enough food, your body will use stored fat for energy. You will lose weight. People who are underweight are also at risk of heart problems and other diseases.

People who are either underweight or obese should talk to a doctor. They may need help to get back to a healthy weight.

Keeping fit and healthy is a good habit to get into!

How Does Food Spoil?

If food is not stored properly it can **spoil**, or go bad. Storing food in these ways can help keep it safe:

- In the refrigerator
- In the freezer
- Sealed in a container
- Stored in a substance that preserves the food

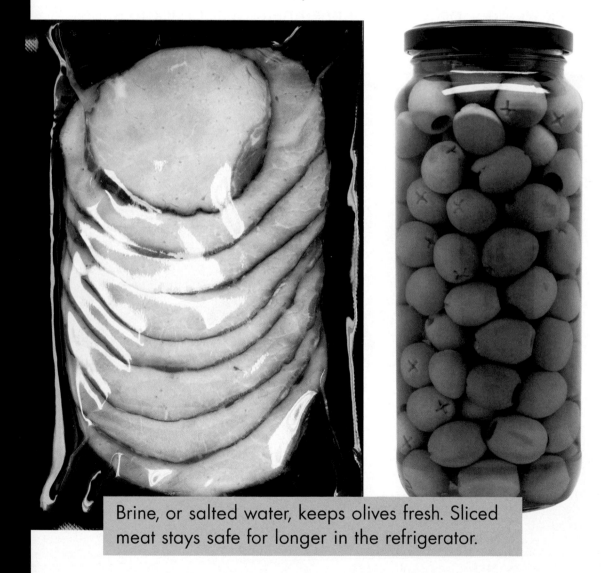

Brine, or salted water, keeps olives fresh. Sliced meat stays safe for longer in the refrigerator.

Sometimes food is not cooked well. Sometimes it is stored incorrectly. Then, **microorganisms** can grow on it. Microorganisms include bacteria and fungus.

What Happens If I Eat Food That's Gone Bad?

If you eat bad food, your tongue may detect this. If you swallow the food, your body will still try to get rid of it. It can do this in two ways. You may vomit. Or you may have diarrhea. Both methods get the microorganisms out of your body as fast as possible!

Having food poisoning can be very painful. It can make your stomach and intestines hurt. To prevent food poisoning, it is important to store and cook food properly. Wash your hands before you touch food. And always check the **"best before"** date.

Even ice creams can give you food poisoning. Make sure an ice cream has not melted, then been refrozen.

Your digestive system is good at keeping you healthy. It takes the goodness from food. It protects you from bad food. It is complex and **efficient**. Make sure you take good care of it!

GLOSSARY

absorb (ab ZORB) — to soak up

"best before" date (best bi FOR date) — the date by which you should eat food

bacteria (bak TIHR ee uh) — the type of tiny organism that can only be seen under a microscope

bile (bile) — the juice produced by the liver that helps digest fat

cell (sel) — the smallest unit of any living thing

decay (di KAY) — to rot

digestion (duh JESS chuhn) — the process of breaking down food so that it can be absorbed into the body

digestive system (duh JESS tiv SISS tuhm) — all the organs that take in, digest food and expel waste

efficient (uh FISH uhnt) — well-organized; produces as little waste as possible

enzyme (en ZIME) — a chemical that speeds up a reaction

esophagus (i SOF uh guhss) — the passage that connects the mouth and stomach

gland (gland) — a structure that releases substances into the body; salivary glands release saliva into the mouth

heartburn (HART burn) — a burning feeling in the chest caused by acid from the stomach splashing up

indigestion (in duh JESS chuhn) — the discomfort caused by difficulty in digesting food

large intestine (larj in TESS tin) — the last section of the digestive system

magnified (MAG nuh fyed) — made bigger

microorganisms (mye kroh OR guh niz uhms) — the tiny creatures that can only be seen under a microscope

nutrients (NOO tree uhnts) — substances that provide nourishment

obese (oh BEESS) — extremely overweight

organ (OR guhn) — a complete part of an animal's or plant's body that carries out a particular job; the heart and lungs are both organs

rectum (REK tuhm) — the lowest part of the large intestine, ending in the anus

saliva (suh LYE vuh) — clear liquid in the mouth

small intestine (smawl in TESS tin) — the longest part of the digestive system; most digestion takes place here

spoil (spoil) — to go off, or turn bad

stomach (STUHM uhk) — a bag where food is stored and partly digested

taste bud (tayst buhd) — the part of the tongue that detects flavor

tissue (TISH oo) — a group of cells that carry out a similar function; groups of tissues make up organs

trillion (TRIL yuhn) — a million million (1,000,000,000,000)

villi (VIL ee) — the finger-like projections in the small intestine

FURTHER INFORMATION

Books

Basic Biology: Body Systems. Denise Walker. Smart Apple Media, 2007.

Break It Down: The Digestive System. Steve Parker. Raintree, 2006.

Exploring the Human Body – The Stomach and Digestion. Carol Ballard. Kidhaven Press, 2005.

Reading Essentials in Science: Nutrition. Alexandra Powe Allred. Perfection Learning, 2005.

Websites to visit

www.mypyramid.gov
United States Department of Agriculture.
This site offers advice on how to eat healthily. It includes interactive games and exercises.

www.nutritionexplorations.org/kids/nutrition-pyramid.asp
Nutrition Exploration: Kids (National Dairy Council)
This site provides information on the different food groups. It contains a range of interactive activities.

www.harcourtschool.com/activity/digest/
Activities based on the digestive system.

http://digestive.niddk.nih.gov/ddiseases/pubs/yrdd/
National Digestive Disease Information.
An in-depth look at the workings of the digestive sytem.

www.kidshealth.org/kid/body/digest_noSW.html
Kids Health: The Real Deal on the Digestive System.
This site explores the journey your food makes after
it is eaten.

INDEX